Grieving Struggles?

Don Barnes

Published by Don Barnes, 2024.

Table of Contents

About the Author

Don is the founder and author of Life Works in Threes!™ E-books. He is a lifelong Texan who has traveled extensively while taking a keen interest in human behavior. His curiosity about life and what drives humans led him to the discovery of how life works in threes. He coined this term as the *Tryune Concept.*

Don attended college on an athletic scholarship and then embarked on a 30-year career in the oil and gas industry. Since the year 2000, he has been a consultant for distributors and manufacturers of various industries. Along the way, he worked on his Tryune discovery in hopes of someday sharing his findings with those struggling unnecessarily... in life. What Don surmised from 40+ years of R&D was that people were struggling unnecessarily because they were not aware that "life works in threes." They, for the most part, have been living their lives <u>by chance</u> rather than <u>by choice,</u> he also discovered.

From this, he began focusing on the "mechanics of life" which shows formulas for success with subjects such as *life, health, money, purpose and so forth.* When people are able to grasp the Tryune Concept, they can apply the formulas with topics that interest them and begin eliminating the struggle. This epiphany is what triggered his Tryune venture and is now on the path of sharing with all who desire to improve on their lives.

Don currently resides in Southern California and Texas while overseeing his businesses and investments.

Life Works in Threes™

When I was a kid growing up, no one sat me down and said, "Okay Don, I'm going to show you how life works so that you can navigate your way through adulthood." I graduated from school, got married and went about my way with the "learn as you go" concept. It was kind of like putting together a backyard swing set without a set of instructions. Lots of frustration and do-overs, for sure!

My discovery of the "triune" word and noticing how things come together in threes is really what set me off on researching that maybe "life comes in three" ...sort of a mechanical approach to managing life, if you will. I combed the libraries and bookstores for information on this and found one book on the subject that was written back in 1951. The author's name was John S. Arant.

What Mr. Arant had to say is this "For lack of a better name, I have called this *The Triangle of Triumph* and therefore, consistent with the name, since most of these conclusions are built on the geometric figure of the triangle." He continued "All Life and all lives are seated in, and circumscribed by, the triangle. The Author and Source and Director of all life is Himself triune in character – Father, Son, and Holy Spirit. Man is of triple nature – body, mind, and spirit – and within those three there are many triangles – desires, development, decay; intellect, will, sensibilities. Of this "paced interlude in the midst of eternity" which we call time there is the triangle of Past, Present, and Future. Space – that limitless and measureless element of the physical universe – is best known in terms of Height, Breadth, and Depth. Try building yourself some triangles along the lines of your Will, your Work, your Way – You will find some interesting angles.

So, for the first time, I realized that life is designed in a mechanical way to come in threes. That means you don't have to rely on wishing and hoping things turn out okay. You can actually look at the three parts that a particular thing is made of and then apply them to get what you're wanting. Like a three-ingredient recipe or a combination lock. With a combination lock, you need the three exact numbers to unlock the lock...otherwise you will continue to struggle.

Some 40 years later, I accumulated things that work in threes and that's when I knew I needed to share this with anyone wanting answers. To have success/harmony in your life, just apply the three parts of an area you're working on, and things will fall into place. I also learned that the recipe for success with just about anything is by doing these three things, consistently – THINK positively, SPEAK positively and ACT positively. For example, if I want to be a successful artist. I would think to myself "I can do this because I have the talent." Then I would speak it this way "Yes, I am working on my art degree and plan to do portraits professionally." Finally, I would act on that by taking art classes and continue crafting my skill. Eventually, I will see the positive results/ success I'm looking for.

Conversely, if I think positively but speak negatively...it will cancel out. Or if I speak positively but have no positive action going on...nothing will happen.

I looked up "How Life Works" and "The Mechanics of Life" and these are really talking about the biology of how our cells work and other chemistry. TRYUNE WORKS! teaches that life is kind of like building blocks. Pick a topic you may be struggling with. See the three parts that topic consists of and then start applying them...on a consistent basis. That will help you overcome the struggle and get you back in harmony/ success with how life works.

For 30+ years I was a golf instructor (by accident). My two kids had some success playing junior golf and so friends and neighbors would ask me to show them and their kids how to play golf successfully. From all of this, I got pretty good at watching golfers on the driving range and could spot right away why they were struggling with hitting bad golf shots. I was able to do that because I knew the three steps to hitting good golf shots. I learned them from studying golf and played for several decades. I "broke the code" for me so to speak.

So now you know that life works in threes. You can live your life *by choice* rather than *by chance* and that my friend... is the key to a fulfilling life.

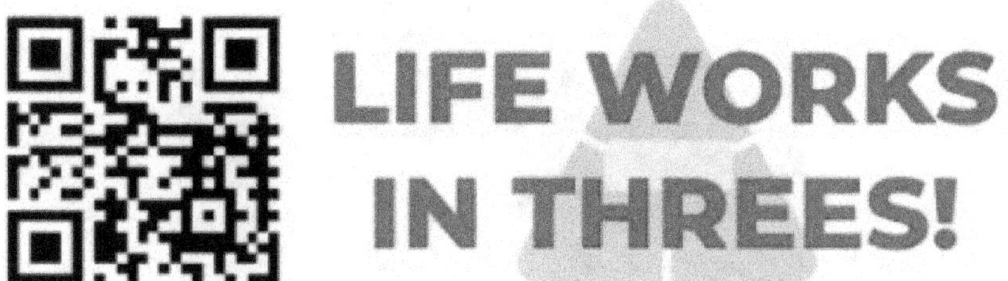
LIFE WORKS
IN THREES!

My sanctuary on the Pacific coast

Introduction

Grieving is a natural and inevitable part of the human experience, a testament to the depth of our emotional connections and the impact of loss. Firstly, it's important to recognize that grief arises not only from the death of a loved one but also from other significant losses such as the end of a relationship, the loss of a job, or even a change in health. These experiences can evoke powerful emotions like sadness, anger, confusion, and even relief, reflecting the complexity of our responses to change and transition in life.

Secondly, grieving allows us to process and make sense of these losses. It provides an opportunity to honor and remember what or whom we've lost, acknowledging their importance in our lives. Through grief, we confront the reality of impermanence and the deep bonds that shape our identities and relationships. This process of reflection and introspection can lead to personal growth, resilience, and a deeper appreciation for the moments and people who enrich our lives.

Furthermore, grieving is a shared human experience that connects us with others. It fosters empathy and understanding, as we recognize that everyone encounters loss at some point in their lives. Supporting one another through grief—whether through listening, offering comfort, or simply being present—strengthens our social bonds and reinforces our sense of community. By acknowledging and accepting grief as a natural part of life, we can embrace its transformative potential and find solace in the collective journey of healing and renewal.

My discovery of the Tryune Concept

Before we dive into grieving struggles and how to overcome them, let me share my discovery of the Tryune Concept and how life works in threes. It all began in the summer of 1982.

I grew up with parents who treated everyone with decency and respect. My three older sisters and I were raised in a home that was "middle-class traditional." We lived in modest homes in different small towns, attended school and church on a regular basis and celebrated all the traditional holidays. Eventually we settled during the spring of 1964 in the big city of Houston, Texas. I'll never forget the vastness of the city and hearing sirens from police cars, fire trucks and ambulances on a regular basis. I was excited and scared at the same time.

Once settled in this fast-paced city, I finished my growing-up years with an academic diploma and sweetheart intact. I got a job, bought a car, got married, bought a house and produced two beautiful babies in a span of about 5 years. Talk about having to grow up fast!

Things went from great in my childhood to absolute misery in my young adulthood. I began to struggle with my job because deep down I just hated what I was doing. This problem created a snowball effect because soon after, my weight, my finances, my relationships, my happiness and everything else worth saving was going down the drain. I eventually hit a level of frustration that I had never experienced before and didn't know how to get out of it. My cry for help was for anyone or anything to come to my rescue. I just ran out of solutions for my situation.

This is when my discovery happened.

One night shortly after my meltdown, while sleeping soundly, the word "triune" began to softly pound in my head like a mantra. I woke up a little startled and decided to go look up the word in my favorite dictionary (this was WAY before Google.) The definition said '**triune** (try-une) – 1) a group of three things; united. 2) Being 3 in 1 such as *humans are mental, physical and spiritual.* I scratched my head, got a glass of water and went back to bed.

The next day while driving around town, I began thinking about things that I was taught in my younger years that came in threes. My Boy Scout manual taught that to have **character**, I needed to be *1) physically strong,* 2) *mentally awake and 3) morally straight.* My high school football coach would say emphatically "If you want to be **a good football player**, you have to be *1) mobile 2) agile and 3) hostile*!" My first sales manager shared with me that to be **a successful salesman**, I needed to have *1) sales skills, 2) product knowledge and 3) a good image.*

"Hmm", I thought, "wonder if there are other examples out there of things that work in threes?" So, some 40 years later, I have researched and discovered that many, many things work in threes. What this message was telling me is that to achieve success or balance in any significant area of my life, the three things that area consisted of had to be present, continuously. That's when I had my epiphany. This discovery was telling me the secret to how life <u>really</u> works...in a mechanical way.

Tryune is a play on the word "triune" as an invitation to "try" this concept. Furthermore, we do not say that life <u>only</u> works in threes. Life also works in ones, twos, fours and so on. What has been observed though is that the many things significant to life, just so happen to come and work in threes. That's what is being shared in this book.

Now, you are about to see 40+ years of research and proof that life works in threes. I did not make up any of these topics. I invite you to research them on the internet to validate what is written here. There are some interesting facts that most of us have never realized...until now

How Life Works in Threes (around 200 examples)

<u>LIFE</u>

Humans consist of *body, mind and soul.*

A human's basic needs are *health, income and provisions.*

A human's basic wants are *comfort, gain and approval.*

Our minds are made up of the *conscious, the subconscious and the unconscious.*

Philosophy explains *the id, the ego and superego.*

Atoms consist of *protons, neutrons and electrons.*

Motion is explained by *three basic laws.*

Science falls under three main branches: *natural, social and formal sciences*

Time is *past, present and future*...at the same time.

Electricity consists of *ohms, amperes and voltage.*

Music's basic elements are *duration, pitch and timbre.*

Democracy is a government *of the people, by the people and for the people.*

U.S. branches of government are *the judicial, the executive and the legislative.*

Armed Forces protect us on *land, air and sea.*

Environmentally, we are asked *to reduce, recycle and re-use.*

The news program gives us *the news, sports and conditions.*

Our days consist of *morning, afternoon and evening.*

Three months in each season of the year

Our main meals are known as *breakfast, lunch and dinner.*

A balanced diet consists of *good proteins, carbohydrates and fats.*

Traditional Family consists of *father, mother, and child(ren)*

<u>SCIENCES</u>

Three major branches of natural science – *(physical, earth/ space and life sciences)*

Three major branches of modern physics - *(classical, relativistic, quantum)*

Three major branches of biology *(botany, zoology, microbiology)*

Three spatial dimensions: *height* (up/down), *width* (left/ right) and *depth* (forwards/backwards)

Three-gauge bosons (photon, gluon, W&Z bosons)

Three types of elementary particles *(leptons, quarks, gauge bosons)*

Three quarks in every proton *(two "up" and one "down")*

Three primary colors of light *(red, green, blue)*

Three color tone properties *(hue, value, chroma)*

Three laws of motion (*Newton's laws*)

Three laws of planetary motion (*Kepler's laws*)

Three layers of the Sun's interior (*core, radiative zone, convective zone*)

Three layers of the Sun's atmosphere (*photosphere, chromosphere, corona*)

Three types of meteorites (*iron, stony iron, stony*)

Three types of galaxy shapes (*elliptical, spiral, irregular*)

Three substances of the universe (*normal matter, 'dark matter', 'dark energy'*)

Three phases of the moon (*new moon, first quarter, full moon*)

Three planetary regions (*temperate, sub-tropical, tropical*)

Three layers of the Earth (*crust, mantle, core*)

Three components of an ecosystem (*producers, consumers, decomposers*)

Three types of rocks (*igneous, sedimentary, metamorphic*)

Three types of fossil fuels (*coal, crude oil, natural gas*)

Three hydrological processes (*evaporation, condensation, precipitation*)

Three basic types of (meteorological) precipitation (*liquid, freezing, frozen*)

Three types of substances *(mono-constituent, multi-constituent, UVCB)*

Three phases of (normal) matter *(solid, liquid, gas)*

Three types of covalent chemical bonds *(single, double and triple bonds)*

Three isotopes of hydrogen *(protium, deuterium, tritium)*

Three atoms in each molecule of water *(two hydrogen atoms and an oxygen atom)*

Three endings to salts *(-ide, -ite, -ate)*

Three requirements for fire *(fuel, oxygen, heat)*

Three nucleotide bases in a genetic codon

Three domains of life *(archaea, bacteria and eukaryotes)*

Three major groups of flowering plants *(monocots, eudicots, magnolids)*

Three major functions that are basic to plant growth and development: *(photosynthesis* [making sugars], *respiration* [metabolizing those sugars], and *transpiration* [water vapor loss]

Three things that the chlorophyll in plants needs for photosynthesis to take place: *(sunlight, carbon dioxide and water)*

Transpiration serves three roles: *(cooling the plant, moving minerals* and *sugars through the plant,* and *maintaining the turgidity pressure* [stiffness] *of the plant's cells)*

Three parts of an insect's body *(head, thorax, abdomen)*

BIOLOGY

Three types of cones in the retina, relating to the three primary colors

Three semi-circular canals in the ear *(lateral, anterior, posterior)*

Three sections in the ear *(outer, middle, inner)*

Three ossicles in the middle ear *(malleus, incus, stapes)*

Three segments to each limb *(proximal, mid, distal)*

Three bones in each arm *(humerus, radius, ulna)*

Three joints in the arm *(shoulder, elbow, wrist)*

Three joints in the leg *(hip, knee, ankle)*

Three joints in the elbow *(humeroulnar, humeroradial, proximal radioulnar)*

Three functional compartments in the knee joint *(the femoropatellar, medial femorotibial* and *lateral femorotibial articulations)*

Three types of fibrous joints *(sutures, gomphoses, syndesmoses)*

Three types of bone in each hand (*carpals, metacarpals, phalanges*)

Three types of bone in each foot (*tarsals, metatarsals, phalanges*)

Three bones (phalanges) in each finger and in each toe (*proximal, intermediate, distal*)

Three layers of skin (*dermis, epidermis, hypodermis*)

Three components of a cell (*cell membrane, nucleus, cytoplasm*)

Three types of blood vessels (*arteries, veins, capillaries*)

Three types of blood cells [*red* (erythrocytes), *white* (leukocytes), *platelets* (thrombocytes)]

Three processes of the intestinal tract (*ingestion, digestion, excretion*)

Three germ layers (*Endoderm, Mesoderm, Ectoderm*)

Three parts of a human tooth (*crown, neck, root*)

Three organs of otolaryngology (*ear, nose, throat*)

Three major body systems (*digestive, circulatory, respiratory*)

Three parts to a neuron: (*soma* [*cell body*], *axon, dendrites*)

Three main parts of the brain (*forebrain, midbrain, hindbrain*)

Three parts of the forebrain *(cerebrum, thalamus, hypothalamus)*

Three parts of the midbrain *(colliculi, tegmentum, cerebral peduncles)*

Three parts of the hindbrain *(cerebellum, pons, medulla)*

Three membranes enclosing the brain *(dura mater, arachnoid, pia mater)*

The brain operates on three levels: *consciously* (for cognitive thought and declarative memory); *subconsciously* (for pre-planned actions and procedural memory); and *unconsciously* (for breathing, heart beating, etc.)

Our conscious mind is fed from three sources: *our senses* (which can be fooled); *our memory* (which is flawed); and *our imagination* (which is inventive)

Three aspects of the human mind *(memory, intellect, will)*

Three parts of the human personality *(id, ego, superego)*

The sum of human capacity consists of three abilities *(thought, word and deed)*

Three times of man *(birth, life, death)*

Three periods of the Gait Cycle *(initial double limb support, single limb support, and terminal double limb support)*

<u>MUSIC</u>

Three types of musical notes *(sharps, flats, naturals)*

Three aspects of a song (*lyrics, melody, rhythm*)

Three types of musical chords (*root, third, fifth*)

MATHEMATICS

Three types of a real number (*positive, negative, zero*)

Three parts to any arithmetic operation: for addition: *augend, addend and sum* - for subtraction: *minuend, subtrahend and difference* - for multiplication: *multiplicand, multiplier and product* - for division: *dividend, divisor and quotient*

Three laws of arithmetic operations (*commutative, associative, distributive*)

Three types of equivalence relation (*reflexivity, symmetry, transitivity*)

Three types of symmetry operations (*translation, rotation, reflection*)

Three geometries (*Euclidean, spherical, hyperbolic*)

The number 3 is the basis of an entire branch of mathematics, called trigonometry (from the Greek *trigonon* "triangle" + *metron* "measure")

Three trigonometric functions (*sine, cosine, tangent*)

Three types of average (*mean, mode, median*)

GRAMMAR

Three logical operators (*AND, OR and NOT*)

Three laws of logic (*identity, noncontradiction, excluded middle*)

Three parts of a logical syllogism (*major premise, minor premise, conclusion*)

Three grammatical parts to a sentence (*subject, verb, complement*)

Three persons in grammar [*1st person* (I/we), *2nd* (you or your), *3rd* (he/she/it/they)]

Three genders in grammar [*masculine* (he/him), *feminine* (she/her), *neuter* (it)]

Three forms of comparison in grammar [*positive, comparative* (more, -er), *superlative* (most, -est)]

Three cases in (English) grammar [*subjective/nominative* (he), *objective/accusative* (him) and *possessive/genitive* (his)]

Three parts of a narrative *(beginning, middle, end)*

Components of an essay *(introduction, body, conclusion)*

Elements of a rhetorical appeal *(ethos, pathos, logos)*

Aspects of a story *(plot, characters, setting)*

<u>RELIGION</u>

The Creator – *omniscient, omnipotent, omnipresent*

Christian God – *Father, Son, Holy Spirit*

Jesus – *The Way, The Truth, The Life*

Ancient Near East- *Qudshu, Astarte, Anat*

Classical Antiquity – Many dieties came in threes

Hinduism – Para Brahman is *Brahma, Visnu, Shiva*

Ancient Celtic Cultures – *many example of triad dieties*

Buddhism – *The three jewels*

Taoism – *The three pure ones*

Islam – *Fear, Hope and Love*

Baha'i - *Intention, Power and Action*

Confucianism – *Benevolence, Wisdom and Courage*

<u>OTHER TRIUNE EXAMPLES</u>

3 Coins in a Fountain

3 Days of the Condor

3 Miles in a League

3 Goals in a Hat Trick

3 Piece Suit

3 Feet in a Yard

3 Books in Lord of the Rings

3 Ring Circus

3 Ships of Christopher Columbus

3 Sheets to the Wind

3 Books in a Trilogy

3 Wheels on a Tricycle

3 Wise Men

3-Legged Race

3 Ring Circus

3-Wheeler

3 Cornered Hat

3 Dimensional

3 Musketeers

3 R's (reading, 'riting, 'rithmatic)

3 Sides of a triangle

3 Races in the Triple Crown (horse racing)

3 Angles in a Triangle

3 Trimesters in a Pregnancy

3 Flavors in Neapolitan Ice Cream

3 Stars in Orion's belt

3 Barleycorns in an Inch

3 Hands on a Clock (with the Seconds Hand)

3 Colors in a Flag

3 Minute Egg

3 Great Pyramids at Giza

3 Holes in a Bowling Ball

3 Colors in a Set of Traffic Lights

3 Minutes in a Boxing Round

3 Teaspoons in a Tablespoon

3 Legs on a Stool

3 Monastic Vows (Obience, Stability, Conversatio Morum)

3 Body Types: Endomorph, Mesomorph, Ectomorph

3 Ring Notebooks

3 Germ layers: Endoderm, Mesoderm, Ectoderm

3 Species of Homo: Homo habilis, Homo erectus, Homo sapiens

3 Basic parts of a camera: Lens, Shutter, Sensor

3 Stages of a Project lifecycle: initiation, planning, execution

The Truth, The Whole Truth and Nothing but the Truth

Life, Liberty and the Pursuit of Happiness

Hear no Evil, See no Evil, Speak no Evil

National motto of France/Haiti: Liberty, Equality, Fraternity

Paper, Rock, Scissors

Ready, Aim, Fire

On Your mark, Get Set, Go

Olympic medals of gold, silver, bronze

Types of joints (ball & socket, hinge, pivot)

Stages of a rocket launch (launch, orbit, re-entry)

Parts of a joke (setup, delivery, punchline)

Primary components of a transistor (emitter, base, collector)

Primary components of an airplane (fuselage, wings, empennage)

Basic components of a computer: CPU, memory, storage

Three phases in the development of technology (*eotechnic* [*mechanical*], *paleotechnic* [*steam-powered*] and *neotechnic* [*electric-powered*]

Communication systems require three components (*transmitter, channel, receiver*)

The list goes on. See if you can find more examples as they are everywhere in our universe. Now that you know that life works in threes (with proof!), we can begin to apply this concept to whatever topics we want.

So, to overcome struggles with grieving, we need to apply the three areas that grieving consists of – ACKNOWLEDGE, EXPRESS and ADJUST. Let's get started!

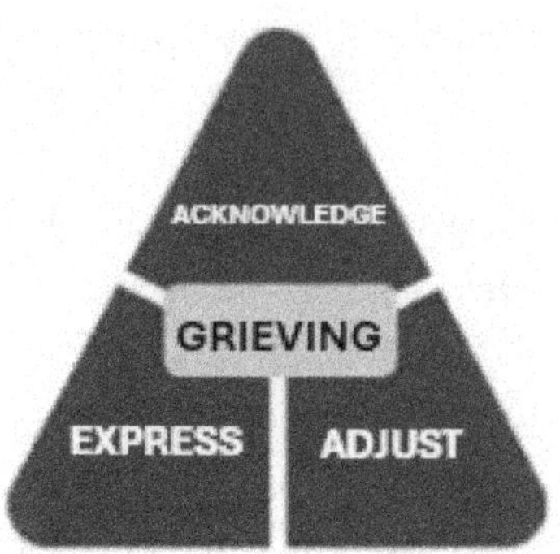
ACKNOWLEDGE
GRIEVING
EXPRESS
ADJUST

GRIEVING

Navigating the grieving process involves understanding three key aspects that can help individuals cope and heal in a healthy manner. Firstly, **acknowledgment** is crucial—recognizing and accepting the reality of the loss. It's okay to feel a range of emotions, from sadness to anger, as each person processes grief differently. Giving oneself permission to experience these feelings without judgment is an essential part of beginning the healing journey.

Secondly, **expression** plays a vital role. Finding healthy outlets to express emotions, such as talking with trusted friends or family members, writing in a journal, or engaging in creative activities like art or music, can be immensely therapeutic. By expressing emotions rather than suppressing them, individuals can gradually come to terms with their loss and find a sense of emotional relief.

Lastly, **adjustment** is about gradually adapting to life without the presence of what or whom has been lost. This involves making practical adjustments, such as establishing new routines or roles, as well as emotional adjustments, like finding ways to remember and honor the person or thing that is no longer physically present. It's important to give oneself time and space to adjust, recognizing that healing from grief is a process that unfolds gradually over time.

Understanding these three keys—*acknowledgment, expression, and adjustment*—can provide a framework for navigating grief in a way that promotes healing and eventual acceptance. Each person's journey through grief is unique, and seeking support from loved ones or professional counselors can also be beneficial in finding comfort and moving forward positively.

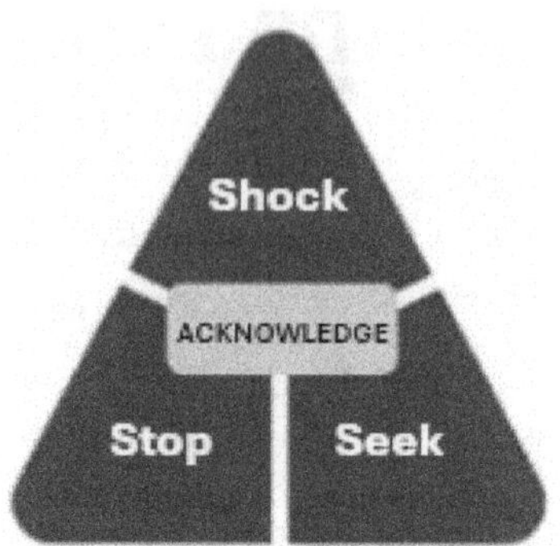

Shock
ACKNOWLEDGE
Stop
Seek

ACKNOWLEDGMENT

Acknowledging the loss of someone is a crucial step in the process of grieving and healing. Firstly, facing the reality of loss allows individuals to begin processing their emotions in a healthy and constructive manner. Denial, on the other hand, involves avoiding or refusing to accept the truth of the loss, which can hinder emotional healing and prolong the grieving process. By acknowledging the loss, individuals open themselves up to experiencing the full range of emotions associated with grief—such as sadness, anger, guilt, and even relief—which are essential for moving forward and finding eventual peace.

Also, acknowledging the loss of someone honors their memory and significance in our lives. It allows us to reflect on the impact they had, the memories shared, and the lessons learned from our relationship with them. This acknowledgment validates the importance of the person who has passed away and reinforces their legacy in our hearts and minds. It also provides an opportunity to celebrate their life, commemorate their achievements, and find comfort in cherished memories.

Finally, acknowledging loss fosters authenticity and emotional resilience. It encourages individuals to confront difficult emotions and challenges, promoting personal growth and inner strength. By acknowledging the reality of loss, individuals can seek support from loved ones or professional counselors, who can provide comfort, guidance, and understanding during the grieving process. Ultimately, embracing the reality of loss with courage and honesty allows individuals to navigate grief more effectively, fostering healing and eventual acceptance while honoring the memory of those we have lost.

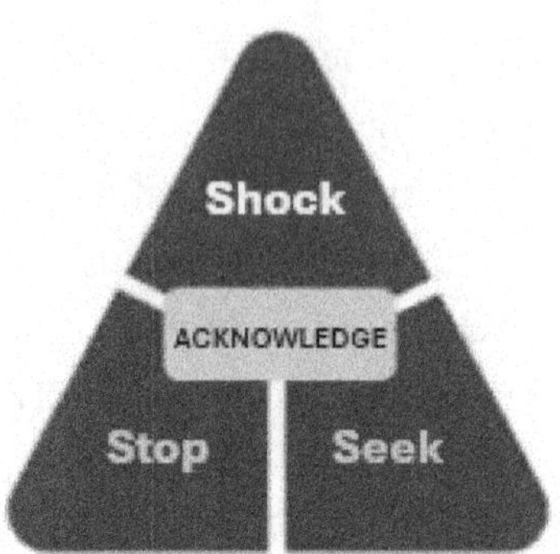
Shock
ACKNOWLEDGE
Stop
Seek

Shock

Experiencing shock is a common and natural response to a significant loss, as it can be overwhelming to process the sudden or unexpected absence of someone dear. Firstly, shock often manifests as a state of disbelief or numbness, where individuals may feel disconnected from reality or emotionally numb. This initial reaction serves as a protective mechanism, allowing individuals to gradually absorb the reality of the loss at a pace that feels manageable. It's important to recognize that shock is a temporary phase and varies in intensity and duration for each person.

Secondly, while shock can provide a temporary buffer against the full impact of grief, it's essential to acknowledge and address underlying emotions as they surface. Suppressing feelings of sadness, anger, or confusion can prolong the grieving process and impact emotional well-being over time. It's okay to seek support from trusted friends, family members, or counselors who can provide comfort, reassurance, and a listening ear during this vulnerable period.

Lastly, navigating through shock involves adjusting to a new reality without the presence of the person who has passed away. This adjustment can be challenging and may involve making practical changes to daily routines, responsibilities, and social interactions. By acknowledging and accepting the emotions that accompany shock—while allowing oneself time to grieve and heal—individuals can gradually integrate the loss into their lives and find ways to honor the memory of their loved one. Embracing self-care practices, engaging in activities that bring comfort and solace, and seeking professional support when needed can all contribute to navigating through shock and moving forward positively in the grieving process.

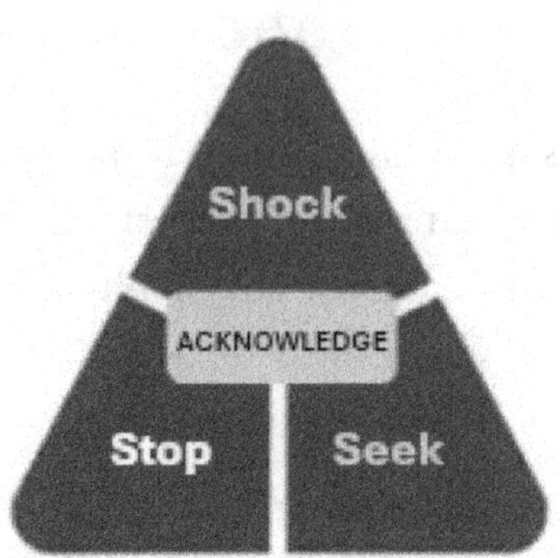
Shock
ACKNOWLEDGE
Stop
Seek

Stop

Taking time to regroup after experiencing the loss of a loved one is crucial for emotional healing and adjustment. Firstly, pausing to regroup allows individuals to acknowledge and process their emotions in a supportive and compassionate manner. Grief can evoke a range of feelings such as sadness, anger, guilt, and even relief, and giving oneself permission to experience and express these emotions is an important part of the healing process. This pause provides an opportunity to reflect on the significance of the person who has passed away, honor their memory, and come to terms with the impact of their absence.

Secondly, regrouping after loss helps individuals to regain a sense of stability and balance amidst the upheaval of emotions and changes. It allows time for self-care and nurturing, which are essential for physical, mental, and emotional well-being during a challenging time. Engaging in activities that promote relaxation, such as spending time in nature, practicing mindfulness or meditation, or participating in hobbies that bring comfort and solace, can provide a sense of grounding and renewal.

Furthermore, stopping to regroup fosters resilience and personal growth. It encourages individuals to assess their current circumstances, identify their needs and priorities, and adjust as necessary. This may involve seeking support from friends, family, or professionals who can offer guidance, empathy, and practical assistance. By taking proactive steps to regroup, individuals can gradually navigate through grief, adapt to life without their loved one, and find ways to move forward with resilience and hope. Each person's journey through grief is unique, and allowing oneself the time and space to regroup is a compassionate and empowering choice on the path toward healing.

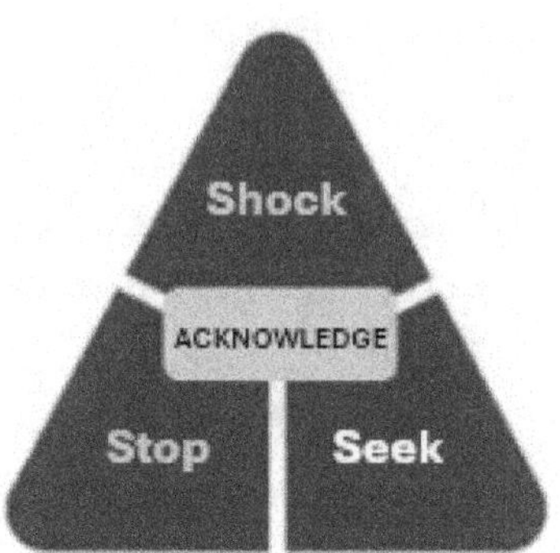
Shock
ACKNOWLEDGE
Stop
Seek

Seek

Seeking out others while going through the loss of a loved one is crucial for emotional support, comfort, and resilience. Connecting with friends, family members, or support groups provides a sense of belonging and reassurance during a difficult time. Sharing memories, emotions, and experiences with others who have also experienced loss can offer validation and understanding, reducing feelings of isolation and loneliness. These connections remind individuals that they are not alone in their journey of grief and can provide comfort through companionship and empathy.

Seeking out others fosters a supportive network that can offer practical assistance and guidance. Friends and family members may help with daily tasks, provide meals, or offer childcare, alleviating some of the burdens and allowing individuals to focus on their emotional well-being. Additionally, trusted individuals can serve as sounding boards for processing feelings and making decisions, offering valuable perspectives and advice based on their own experiences. This support network becomes a source of strength and resilience, empowering individuals to navigate through grief with greater emotional stability and confidence.

Finally, seeking out others encourages open communication and healthy coping mechanisms. Expressing feelings and emotions verbally can be cathartic and therapeutic, helping to release tension and promote healing. Listening to the stories and perspectives of others who have navigated similar experiences can provide insight and validation, offering new perspectives on grief and coping strategies. By actively engaging with supportive relationships, individuals can build resilience, find comfort in shared experiences, and cultivate a sense of hope and optimism for the future. Ultimately, seeking out others during the loss of a loved one underscores the importance of human connection in the healing process, providing essential emotional and practical support that contributes to a more positive and meaningful journey through grief.

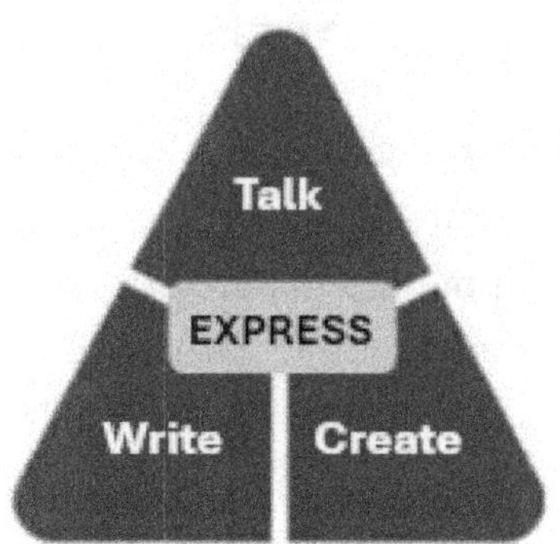
Talk
EXPRESS
Write
Create

EXPRESSION

After experiencing loss, there are various ways individuals can express grief that resonate personally and help in the healing process. Firstly, **creative outlets** such as art, writing, or music offer powerful means to externalize emotions. Painting, drawing, or creating collages can visually represent feelings of sorrow, longing, or even gratitude for the time spent with a loved one. Writing poetry, journals, or letters to the departed can serve as therapeutic avenues to process thoughts and emotions, providing a sense of closure or connection.

Secondly, **physical activity** can be a constructive way to manage grief. Engaging in activities like walking, jogging, yoga, or even gardening can help release pent-up emotions and alleviate stress. Physical exercise boosts endorphins, which can improve mood and provide a temporary distraction from grief. Additionally, being in nature or participating in outdoor activities can offer a sense of peace and renewal, fostering a connection with the natural world that may bring comfort during difficult times.

Thirdly, **community involvement** provides opportunities to channel grief into positive action. Volunteering for causes that were meaningful to the departed or participating in support groups can create a sense of purpose and connection. Helping others who are also experiencing loss can foster empathy and understanding, while receiving support from others who share similar experiences can provide comfort and validation. Engaging with community rituals or ceremonies, such as memorial services or tribute events, allows individuals to honor their loved one publicly and commemorate their life in a meaningful way.

Each person's journey through grief is unique, and exploring different methods of expression can help individuals find what resonates most deeply and supports their path toward healing.

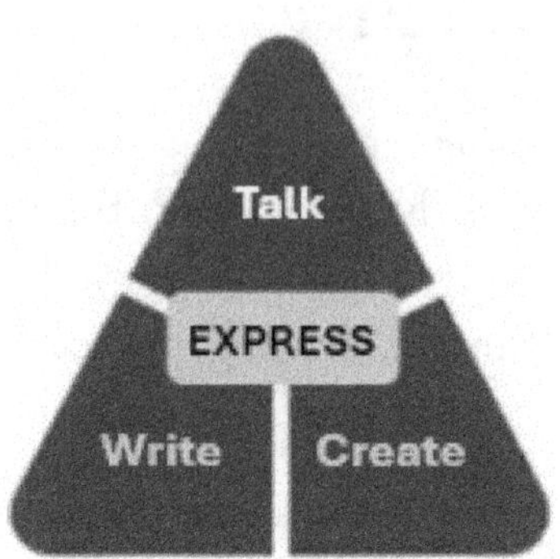

Talk
EXPRESS
Write
Create

Talk

Talking with others while grieving is incredibly important for emotional healing and support during a challenging time. Sharing feelings, memories, and experiences with trusted friends, family members, or counselors provides a sense of relief and validation. Verbalizing emotions can help individuals process grief more effectively, allowing them to release pent-up emotions and find comfort in knowing that their thoughts and feelings are heard and understood. This open communication fosters connection and empathy, strengthening relationships and providing reassurance that one is not alone in their journey of grief.

Talking with others offers an opportunity for reflection and storytelling, which can be therapeutic and healing. Sharing memories and anecdotes about the loved one who has passed allows individuals to honor their legacy and keep their spirit alive in conversation. This act of remembrance helps to preserve the bond with the departed and provides a sense of continuity amidst the loss. Furthermore, talking with others can provide new perspectives and insights into grief and coping strategies. Friends and family members who have navigated similar experiences may offer advice, support, and practical suggestions for managing grief, which can be invaluable during times of emotional turmoil.

Finally, talking with others facilitates a sense of community and belonging. Expressing vulnerability and receiving empathy from others strengthens social bonds and creates a supportive network of individuals who can offer comfort and companionship throughout the grieving process. This sense of community provides a safe space for individuals to express their feelings authentically and receive the emotional support needed to navigate through grief with resilience and strength. By fostering open and compassionate communication, talking with others becomes a powerful tool for healing, promoting emotional well-being, and fostering a sense of hope and renewal in the face of loss.

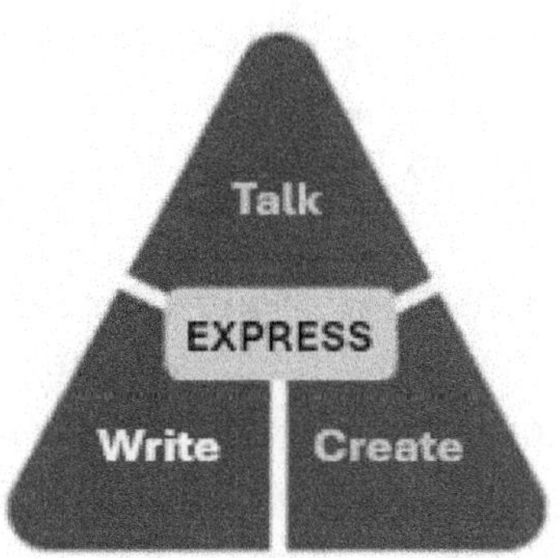
Talk
EXPRESS
Write
Create

Write

Writing about your loss can be an incredibly helpful and therapeutic practice during the grieving process. Journaling allows individuals to express complex emotions and thoughts in a private and introspective space. Writing about your loss provides an outlet to explore feelings of sadness, anger, guilt, or confusion that may arise after the death of a loved one. It can be a cathartic experience, helping to release pent-up emotions and reduce emotional distress. This process of self-expression through writing promotes emotional clarity and self-awareness, allowing individuals to gain insight into their grief journey and begin to make sense of their feelings.

Writing about your loss preserves memories and honors the life of a departed loved one. Reflecting on shared experiences, cherished moments, and lessons learned from the relationship can be a comforting way to keep their memory alive. Writing can serve as a tribute to the person who has passed, capturing their essence and impact on your life in words. This act of remembrance helps individuals to feel connected to their loved one and fosters a sense of continuity amidst the pain of loss.

Also, writing about your loss provides a tangible record of your journey of grief, documenting the highs and lows of your emotional experience over time. Reviewing previous entries can track progress, identify patterns of healing, and recognize moments of growth and resilience. Additionally, writing can serve as a tool for setting intentions, processing challenges, and finding moments of gratitude or hope amid grief. Whether through journaling, writing letters to the departed, or composing poetry or prose, the act of putting thoughts into words can be a powerful therapeutic tool that supports healing, self-discovery, and emotional well-being during the grieving process.

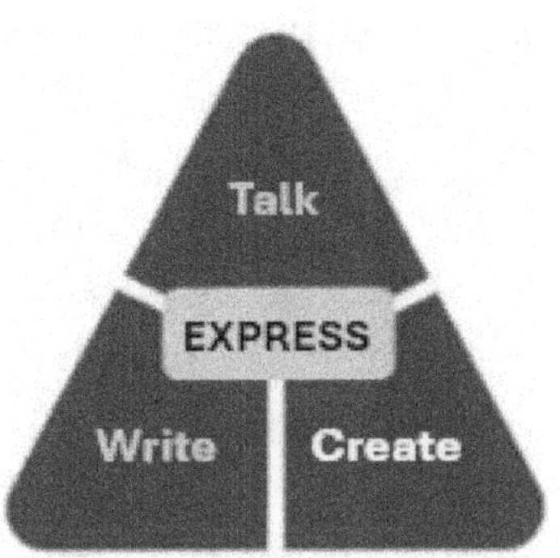
Talk
EXPRESS
Write
Create

Create

Creating while going through loss can be a deeply meaningful and therapeutic way to navigate the grieving process. Engaging in creative activities such as art, music, or crafting offers a constructive outlet for expressing emotions that may be difficult to articulate verbally. Creativity allows individuals to externalize feelings of grief, sadness, or even joy and gratitude for the time spent with the departed loved one. Whether painting, sculpting, playing an instrument, or writing poetry, the act of creating can provide a sense of release and catharsis, helping to alleviate emotional distress and promote healing.

Creating can serve as a form of tribute or memorial to honor the life and legacy of the loved one who has passed away. Channeling grief into creative endeavors allows individuals to celebrate their memories, values, and impact on their lives. For example, creating a scrapbook, photo album, or digital collage featuring cherished moments and mementos can preserve the essence of the person who has passed and provide comfort through the act of remembrance. Engaging in creative projects that pay homage to their passions or interests can also be a meaningful way to feel connected to their spirit and continue their legacy.

The process of creating offers a sense of purpose and accomplishment during a time of profound loss. Setting aside dedicated time for creative expression provides a constructive focus and an opportunity to channel emotions into something positive and tangible. This sense of productivity can boost self-esteem, promote resilience, and foster a sense of agency amidst the overwhelming emotions of grief. Additionally, sharing creative works with others—whether through exhibitions, performances, or simply sharing with friends and family—can create connections, evoke empathy, and provide a source of comfort and support from the community. Ultimately, engaging in creative activities while grieving not only facilitates emotional healing but also celebrates the unique bond shared with the departed loved one, fostering a sense of continuity and hope for the future.

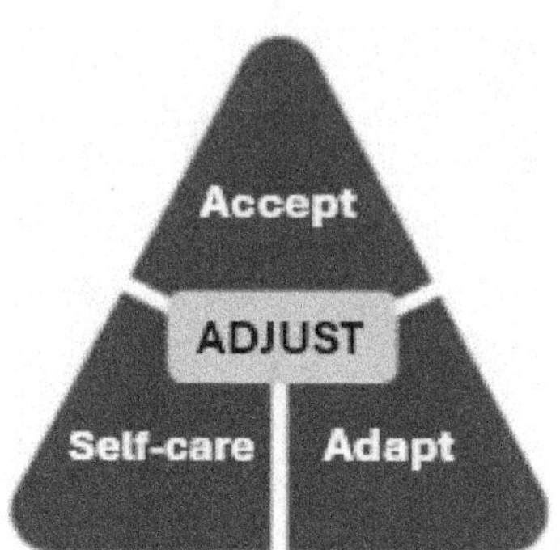
Accept
ADJUST
Self-care
Adapt

ADJUST

Adjusting during a loss involves navigating through a period of profound emotional upheaval with care and self-compassion. Firstly, **accepting** is key. Recognizing and accepting the reality of the loss is essential for beginning the process of adjustment. This involves allowing yourself to experience the full range of emotions that come with grief—whether it's sadness, anger, guilt, or even moments of relief. Giving yourself permission to feel these emotions without judgment is a crucial step towards healing.

Secondly, **self-care** plays a pivotal role in adjustment. Taking care of your physical, emotional, and mental well-being during this challenging time is essential. This includes getting enough rest, eating nourishing meals, and engaging in activities that bring comfort and solace. Practicing mindfulness, meditation, or relaxation techniques can help manage stress and promote a sense of calm amidst the turmoil of grief. Additionally, seeking support from loved ones, counselors, or support groups can provide a sense of connection and reassurance, reminding you that you're not alone in your journey.

Lastly, **adaptation** involves making practical adjustments to life without the presence of the loved one who has passed away. This may include reevaluating routines, roles, and responsibilities, and finding new ways to navigate daily challenges. It's okay to take things one step at a time and adjust gradually to the changes that come with loss. Flexibility and patience with yourself are key as you find ways to honor the memory of your loved one while moving forward with resilience and hope. Adjusting during a loss is a personal and ongoing process that unfolds differently for everyone, and by embracing acknowledgment, self-care, and adaptation, you can navigate grief with grace and compassion.

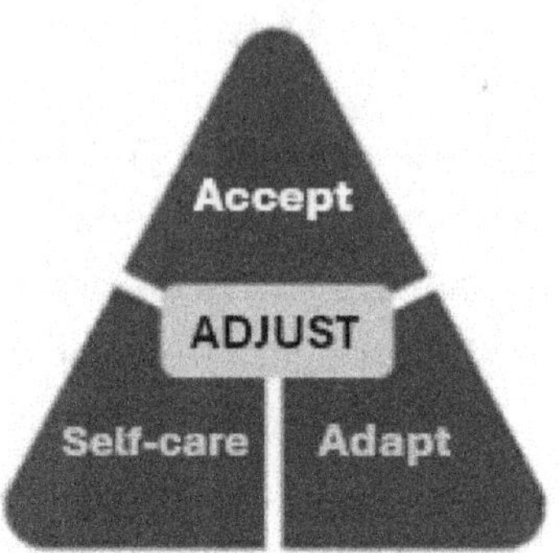

Accept
ADJUST
Self-care
Adapt

Accept

Accepting a significant loss is a profound journey that involves acknowledging, processing, and eventually finding peace with the reality of the situation. Acceptance begins with acknowledgment—recognizing and coming to terms with the fact that the loss has occurred. This may involve facing the pain, sadness, and even disbelief that accompanies the initial stages of grief. It's normal to experience a range of emotions during this time, and allowing yourself to feel them without judgment is an important part of the healing process.

Perspective plays a crucial role in accepting a big loss. It involves gradually shifting your focus from the overwhelming sense of loss to finding meaning and understanding in the experience. This may include reflecting on the lessons learned, the impact of the relationship or situation, and the ways in which it has shaped your life. Finding moments of gratitude for the time spent with the person or the experiences shared can help in reframing the loss as part of a larger narrative of growth and resilience.

Self-compassion is essential in the journey of acceptance. It involves treating yourself with kindness, patience, and understanding as you navigate through the complexities of grief. Practicing self-care, setting realistic expectations, and seeking support from loved ones or professionals can provide comfort and reassurance during this vulnerable time. Acceptance does not mean forgetting or moving on from the loss—it means finding a sense of peace and closure while honoring the memory of what or whom you have lost. By embracing acknowledgment, gaining perspective, and practicing self-compassion, you can gradually come to accept a big loss and find a path forward with strength and resilience.

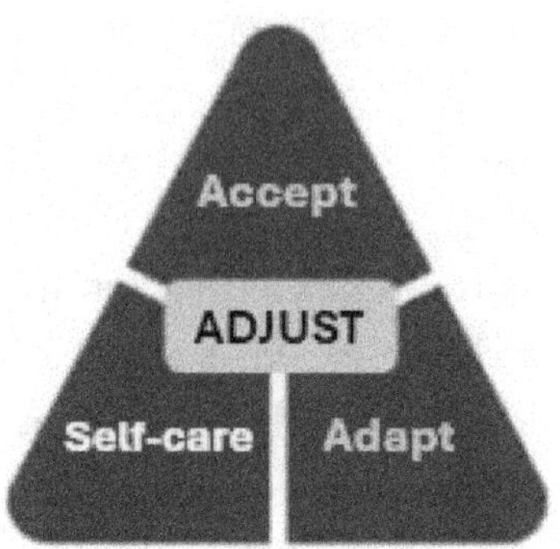

Accept
ADJUST
Self-care
Adapt

Self-care

Self-care is of utmost importance when navigating the grieving process, as it provides a foundation of support and resilience during a time of emotional upheaval. **Physical self-care** involves attending to your body's needs. This includes getting adequate rest, nourishing yourself with balanced meals, and engaging in gentle exercise or activities that promote relaxation. Taking care of your physical well-being can help alleviate stress, improve mood, and provide a sense of stability amidst the turbulence of grief.

Emotional self-care focuses on nurturing your emotional well-being. It's important to give yourself permission to feel and express your emotions, whether it's sadness, anger, guilt, or moments of peace and acceptance. Engaging in activities that bring you comfort and solace—such as journaling, meditating, or spending time in nature—can help process emotions and provide a sense of calm. Seeking support from loved ones, support groups, or a therapist can also offer validation and guidance as you navigate through the complexities of grief.

Mental self-care involves managing your thoughts and cognitive processes during grief. This may include practicing mindfulness or relaxation techniques to quiet the mind, challenging negative self-talk or unrealistic expectations, and allowing yourself time to grieve without rushing the healing process. Engaging in hobbies or activities that stimulate your mind and bring enjoyment can also provide a welcome distraction and promote mental clarity. By prioritizing self-care in all its forms—physical, emotional, and mental—you create a nurturing environment that supports healing, resilience, and eventual acceptance during the grieving process. Taking care of yourself allows you to honor your own needs and well-being while navigating the profound journey of grief with compassion and strength.

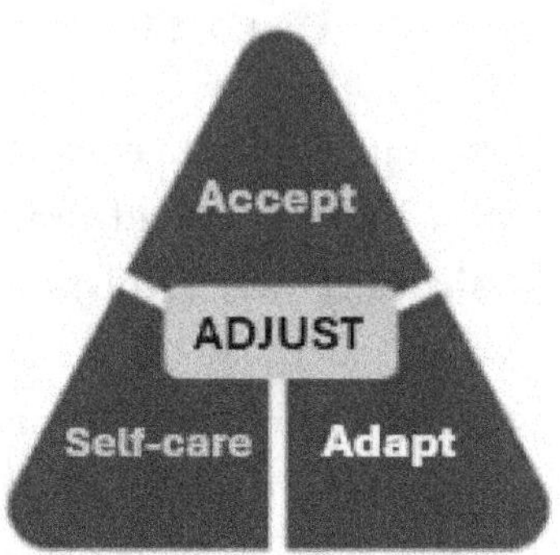
Accept
ADJUST
Self-care
Adapt

Adapt

Adapting to a new lifestyle after experiencing a significant loss is an essential part of the healing process. **Acknowledging the need for adaptation** is key. Recognizing that life has changed and embracing the reality of loss allows individuals to begin adjusting their routines, priorities, and perspectives. This acknowledgment may involve letting go of expectations of how life "should" be and embracing the present moment with compassion and resilience. Understanding that adaptation is a gradual process can alleviate pressure and allow for flexibility in navigating through grief.

Finding a new sense of purpose and meaning in life post-loss is crucial. This involves exploring activities, hobbies, or goals that bring fulfillment and joy in the absence of the loved one. Engaging in meaningful pursuits—whether it's volunteering, pursuing creative endeavors, or connecting with others in new ways—can provide a sense of purpose and direction during a time of uncertainty. Finding ways to honor the memory of the person who has passed while carving out a new path forward fosters resilience and strengthens emotional well-being.

Seeking support and connection plays a vital role in adapting to a new lifestyle after loss. Building a support network of friends, family members, or support groups who can offer empathy, encouragement, and practical assistance can provide a sense of belonging and reassurance. Connecting with others who have experienced similar losses can offer insights, validation, and shared understanding, promoting healing and resilience. Additionally, seeking professional guidance from counselors or therapists can provide personalized strategies and tools to navigate through grief and adjust to life changes effectively.

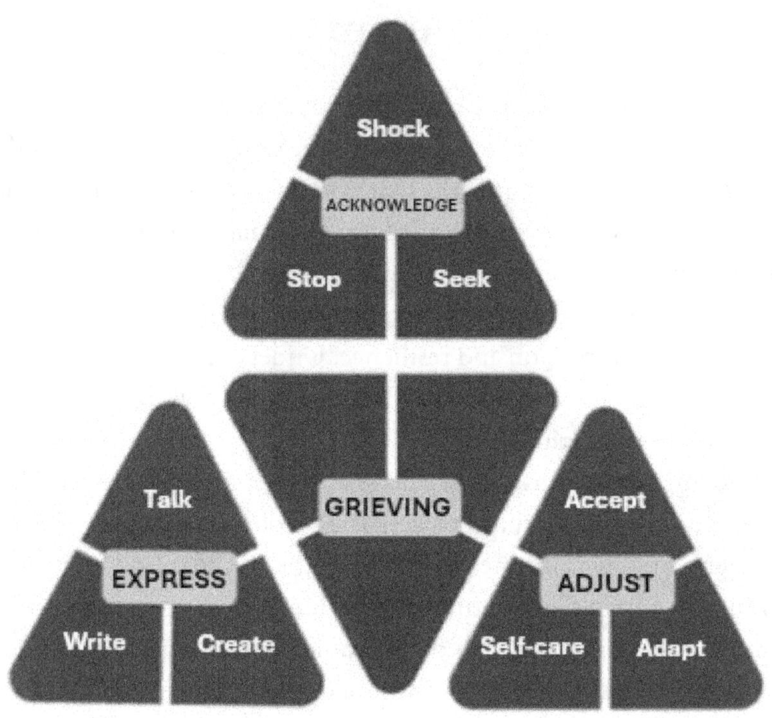

Shock
ACKNOWLEDGE
Stop
Seek
Talk
EXPRESS
Write
Create
GRIEVING
Accept
ADJUST
Self-care
Adapt

SUMMARY

Experiencing loss is a universal part of the human experience and recognizing that everyone goes through it at some point can provide comfort and perspective during difficult times. **Acknowledging the universality of loss** helps normalize the emotions and challenges that accompany grief. Whether it's the death of a loved one, the end of a relationship, or other significant life changes, knowing that others have walked similar paths can reduce feelings of isolation and loneliness. This shared experience underscores the resilience of the human spirit and highlights our capacity to support one another through empathy and understanding.

Finding solidarity in shared experiences can be empowering. Knowing that others have faced and navigated through grief can offer hope and encouragement during moments of despair. Connecting with friends, family, or support groups who have experienced similar losses can provide a sense of validation and companionship. Sharing stories, memories, and coping strategies can offer new perspectives and insights, reinforcing the idea that you are not alone in your journey through grief.

Seeking support from others strengthens social bonds and reinforces a sense of community. Whether through conversations, shared activities, or simply being present for one another, the support of loved ones can provide emotional comfort and practical assistance during challenging times. Additionally, professional counselors or therapists can offer guidance, tools, and strategies to navigate through grief effectively. By reaching out and connecting with others, individuals can find solace in the understanding that grief is a natural and shared experience, and that there are resources and compassionate companionship available to help them through their healing journey.

Invitation

"Expecting the unexpected" can be a valuable mindset when facing the possibility of loss, as it prepares individuals to cope more effectively with the shock and upheaval that often accompany such events. **Mental preparedness** involves recognizing that life can be unpredictable and that unforeseen circumstances may arise. This mindset allows individuals to develop a level of resilience and flexibility, enabling them to respond more calmly and thoughtfully when faced with sudden changes or tragic news. By acknowledging the uncertainty of life, individuals can cultivate a sense of readiness to adapt and cope with challenging situations.

Emotional readiness involves accepting that difficult events may occur and allowing oneself to process a range of emotions, including shock, sadness, and disbelief, when they arise. This acceptance does not diminish the impact of the loss but rather provides a foundation for emotional resilience and self-compassion during times of crisis. It encourages individuals to lean on their support networks, seek professional guidance if needed, and engage in self-care practices that promote emotional well-being. By embracing the reality that life can bring unexpected challenges, individuals can approach loss with greater clarity and inner strength.

Practical preparedness involves making necessary arrangements and plans, such as updating legal documents, discussing end-of-life wishes with loved ones, or having emergency contact information readily available. Taking proactive steps to prepare for the unexpected can alleviate some of the stress and confusion that may accompany a sudden loss. It allows individuals to focus on supporting themselves and their loved ones emotionally, rather than becoming overwhelmed by logistical concerns. By expecting the unexpected and taking proactive measures to prepare, individuals can navigate through loss with greater resilience, preparedness, and a sense of empowerment in the face of life's uncertainties.

When you're with someone who is sharing their struggles with you...just smile at him/her and give them one of these. He/she will ask "What is that?" Then simply reply "Life Works in Threes."

Other titles coming out:

- Weight Struggles?
- Abundance Struggles?
- Parenting Struggles?
- Life Struggles?
- Purpose Struggles?
- Happiness Struggles?
- Sales Struggles?
- Speaker Struggles?
- Time Struggles?
- Network Struggles?
- Marriage Struggles?
- Divorce Struggles?
- Money Struggles?
- Career Struggles?
- Dating Struggles?
- Caretaker Struggles?
- Forgiveness Struggles?
- Romance Struggles?
- Success Struggles?
- Golf Struggles?
- Workplace Struggles?
- Stress Struggles?
- Shame/Guilt Struggles?
- Addiction Struggles?

Quotes about Grieving

"Grief is the price we pay for love." - Queen Elizabeth II

"Grief is like the ocean; it comes on waves ebbing and flowing. Sometimes the water is calm, and sometimes it is overwhelming. All we can do is learn to swim." - Vicki Harrison

"Grief is not a disorder, a disease or a sign of weakness. It is an emotional, physical and spiritual necessity, the price you pay for love. The only cure for grief is to grieve." - Earl Grollman

"The reality is that you will grieve forever. You will not 'get over' the loss of a loved one; you will learn to live with it. You will heal and you will rebuild yourself around the loss you have suffered." - Elizabeth Kubler-Ross

"There is no right way to grieve; there is only your way." - Unknown

Grief can stem from various sources, and it's a natural response to loss or significant change. Some common sources of grieving include:

1. **Death of a loved one**: Losing a family member, friend, or pet can trigger profound grief.
2. **End of a relationship**: Whether through breakup, divorce, or separation, the loss of a significant relationship can be deeply painful.
3. **Loss of health**: Facing a serious illness, disability, or chronic condition can lead to grieving the loss of good health and a sense of normalcy.
4. **Job loss or financial instability**: Losing a job, experiencing financial hardship, or significant changes in financial status can cause grief over lost stability or identity tied to career.
5. **Miscarriage or infertility**: Struggles with fertility, miscarriage, or stillbirth can lead to grief over the loss of a hoped-for child and the dreams associated with parenthood.
6. **Loss of a home or relocation**: Moving away from a familiar place or losing a home due to disaster or financial reasons can trigger feelings of loss and displacement.
7. **Loss of a pet**: The death or loss of a beloved animal companion can cause significant grief, especially for those who view pets as family members.
8. **Loss of a cherished dream or goal**: Failing to achieve a long-held aspiration, such as career ambitions, educational goals, or personal dreams, can lead to grieving the loss of that future.
9. **End of a significant phase of life**: Graduating from

school, retiring from a career, or experiencing other major life transitions can bring about grief over the end of a familiar chapter.

10. **Traumatic experiences**: Survivors of trauma, abuse, or violence may grieve the loss of safety, trust, or innocence.

Grief is a complex emotional process that can vary widely in intensity and duration depending on the individual and the circumstances. It's important to recognize that grieving is a natural response to loss and that everyone experiences it differently.

I remember clearly, 36 years ago, standing by my father's bedside and watching him go to sleep forever. After hugs from my mother and nurses...I walked outside of the hospital and looked in disbelief that the world was still going on. People were walking and talking. Cars were going back and forth on the freeway and planes were flying in the air.

I don't know. I guess I thought the world should stop and recognize that I had just lost my father forever. It still baffles me today that the world doesn't stop when we experience a loss. What a damn shame.

Myths about Grieving

"Grieving should last about a year."

Grieving is different for everyone. There is no specific time frame on this.

"It's important to be "strong" in the face of a loss."

Feeling sad, frightened, or lonely is a normal reaction to loss. Crying doesn't mean you are weak. You don't need to "protect" your family or friends by putting on a brave front. Showing your true feelings can help them and you.

"Moving on with your life means forgetting about your loss."

Moving on means you've accepted your loss—but that's not the same as forgetting. You can move on with your life and keep the memory of someone or something you lost as an important part of you. In fact, as we move through life, these memories can become more and more integral to defining the people we are.

"The pain will go away faster if you ignore it."

Trying to ignore your pain or keep it from surfacing will only make it worse in the long run. For real healing, it is necessary to face your grief and actively deal with it.

"If you don't cry it means you aren't sorry about the loss."

Crying is a normal response to sadness, but it's not the only one. Those who don't cry may feel the pain just as deeply as others. They may simply have other ways of showing it.

When someone is struggling with a particular area or two, chances are they are "out of balance" with how life works. How does life work? Life works in threes.

If you're interested in personal topics like life, health, money or business topics like sales, time management and public speaking...Life Works in Threes! can shed some light on creating success in those areas.

The definition of TRIUNE is a group of three things; united. Being three in one, such as - humans are *mental, physical* and *spiritual beings*. The word TRYUNE is a play of the word TRIUNE, encouraging all to try this concept and help eliminate struggling unnecessarily.

LifeWorksInThrees.com